John Davies
2000

First published 1996
Second edition with revisions 1999
© Wooden Books Ltd 1999

Published by Wooden Books Ltd.
Walkmill, Cascob, Presteigne, Powys, Wales LD8 2NT

British Library Cataloguing in Publication Data
Martineau, John, 1967-
Mazes and Labyrinths

A CIP catalogue record for this book is
available from the British Library

ISBN 0 9525862 1 5

Printed and bound in Great Britain by
the Cromwell Press, Trowbridge, Wiltshire

MAZES

AND

LABYRINTHS

IN GREAT BRITAIN

written and illustrated

by

John Martineau

To my mother, Tess

In this book, to aid comprehension of the designs, most are shown with the entrance at the bottom of the page.

Other good books on Mazes and Labyrinths currently in print are W.H. Matthews classic text and Nigel Pennick's book. A Journal on the subject is Caerdroia, edited by Jeff Saward.

The Archbishop's Maze, Grey's Court, Oxfordshire

CONTENTS

MAZES

Beware!
You *can* get lost

TROY TOWN, SCILLY ISLES

This book treats mazes as designs in which you can get lost. Choices may be offered to the walker and some paths may not lead to the goal. Labyrinths, by contrast, take the walker on a journey to the centre.

Troy Town, on the Scilly Isles, is the only ancient stone and boulder labyrinth in the British Isles. The diagram opposite is schematic and does not show the actual boulders which denote the shape. The construction is about sixteen feet across and overlooks the sea.

In Norway, where more lore exists concerning the use of these seaside designs, fishermen and sailors would walk labyrinths to ensure favourable winds and catches, and also to entrap smägubbar, gremlins or little people.

Few ancient mazes and labyrinths retain the same design over the centuries. Reputedly built by the lighthouse-keeper, Amor Clarke, in 1729, Troy Town was altered in 1986 and again in 1989. The version shown here does offer a small choice near the centre, but happily you still cannot actually fail to reach home.

17ᵀᴴ CENTURY MANUSCRIPT MAZE

This maze appears in early collections and is a good example of the increasing inventiveness and variation around the classical form which characterised the seventeenth and eighteenth centuries.

Upon entering the maze, the aspirant chooses one of two paths, creating a sense of excitement, fear and trepidation. In fact, delightfully, both routes lead to the centre.

A textbook example of good design, the circle here is elegantly and symmetrically divided into eight, and the graphic displays a wonderful balance between line and curve, light and dark.

Mazes with two solutions are quite rare. The only surviving ancient turf labyrinth in Germany has two entrances, a linden tree at its centre and is associated with lovers, dancers, sprinters and shoemakers, all themes which are often found around these engaging forms.

HAMPTON COURT

The Hampton Court maze is a true maze - it is possible to get quite lost! The present hedges were planted in 1690 and may be even older than that.

At least twelve mazes following the Hampton Court route have been built in the British Isles and over half a million people now walk the original each year. The design was very ahead of its time - it includes an 'island', a length of hedge in no way connected to the outer perimeter, making it much harder to solve (*see pages 10 - 12*).

Go in, turn left, right twice, and then left four times to reach the centre. That makes seven turns.

Show below is a near copy to be found under the west tower of St. Helena and St. Mary's church, Bourn, Cambridgeshire. It dates from 1875. In 1912 the font was suddenly moved on top of the maze, making the path impossible to walk.

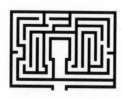

ADAM ISLIP'S DESIGN

A Renaissance publication, *The Orchard and the Garden*, written by Adam Islip in 1602 contains the maze-like labyrinth shown opposite. An arresting design with four square circuits and five circular, it also boasts four secret triangular islands. The total number of circuits is nine.

The theme of this pattern may later have been used by William Waldorf Astor who in 1905 planted a hedge maze very similar to this design at Hever Castle in Kent. The maze is still there and marks the place where Henry VIII once courted Anne Boleyn. A stone labyrinth, also based on this design, can be found at Pahaluoto in Finland.

The design is one way of squaring a circle, where a circle (representing Heaven) and a square (Earth) are unified in an intelligent manner. Here, various aspects of the circular Heavens are explored, but then, in order to actually reach the Centre, the corners of the Earth have to be travelled before the seeker finds the centre.

If you are very careless it is just about possible to get lost.

HATFIELD HOUSE

The yew maze at Hatfield House was planted in 1840. Situated to the east of the house, it is said to stand on the site of an earlier design. There are two entrances, one on the north side and one the south side, which lead respectively to the west and the east sides of the central enclosure.

Once you cross the enclosure, you effectively begin a new maze to find your way out; you are not retracing your steps, and Ariadne's thread will be of no use.

There are no 'islands' at in the Hatfield maze, every element of the design is in some way connected to the outside edge. This means that an ancient trick known as the 'Hand on Wall' method will work here - just slavishly follow the wall with your left hand, groping your way round corners and turning wherever your hand leads you, and you will eventually find the centre, and the exit.

This means that although superficially there seem to be dead ends here, on another level there are none. Mazes such as this can in fact be seen as labyrinths once you have the key.

CHEVENING

By the nineteenth century the process of separation between the physical sciences and the metaphysical sciences was nearly complete in the west. Thus, instead of a path being simply something to follow in order to experience certain things in a certain order and thus reach the centre, the route became confusing.

Some mazes, such as Hatfield House, could be solved by the 'Hand on Wall' method (*described on the previous page*). The maze shown opposite, however, cannot be solved in such a way. It is one of three such mazes designed by Earl Stanhope in the 1820's. An excellent mathematician, he realised that if elements of the design were isolated as 'islands', and not secured to the outer perimeter, then the popular methods of the day would not give the solution. The Hampton Court maze, dating to 1690 (*see page 6*), is the first example of this technique.

This new development made the centre harder to discover and increased the number of people who could not find it.

CHATSWORTH HOUSE

The maze at Chatsworth House was planted in 1962 to an earlier design and stands on the site of the earlier Great Stove glasshouse, designed by Paxton. It is a magical, subtle and beautiful place, with four framed entrances and a small, sweet, central enclosure.

Unusually, the route can be wrongly taken almost even before the centre is sought. Of the four possible entrances into the maze, only one will prove fruitful. This is a feature unique to Chatsworth and reminds the walker of the idea that the right road may need to be chosen from the very start if the preferred destination is to be gained.

There are five circular paths in the design of this maze, with only four of them complete, the fifth being interupted by the linear perimeter. Thus, although the design seems to square the circle, it is actually rectangular in plan, measuring an overall 35 by 41 yards.

LEEDS CASTLE

The maze shown opposite was opened at Leeds Castle, Kent, in 1988. Laid out in yew, the design contains a multitude of islands and is quite a challenge. The successful explorer leaves through an underground grotto, caves and a secret passage.

The design has various echoes of traditional design, and many departures too. Based on seven concentric circles contained within a square, there are numerous solutions, none of them particularly meaningful, but all good fun! The quickest route to the centre is obtained by turning right five times, then second right, left then immediately right, and then finally carrying straight on.

One of the most disorientating things about modern mazes is the allegorical message that it is possible to get lost and fail on the journey to the centre, that the designer of the path is out to trick you and keep you lost, going round in circles. Also, as if failing to reach the centre wasn't bad enough in itself, the desperate hopeful may very possibly never be able to get out of this nightmare again. What fun!

LABYRINTHS

Just follow
the path!

STRAIGHT LINES AND CIRCLES

The common classical labyrinth has seven coils and is shown opposite (*bottom right*) and again on page 31. The top left image opposite shows the standard spiral meander. Both designs are extremely ancient and are widely found all over the world. Both speak of the relation between line and curve.

To get from one to the other, start with two units of a spiral meander (*top left*), imagining it to be made of stretchy stuff. Holding the right edge rigid, pull the left edge out and round one eighth of a circle (*top centre*), then one quarter (*top right*), then one half (*bottom left*) and finally right around to create the labyrinth. The classical seven-coil design is thus already lurking in the spiral meander.

The importance of seven in the ancient world cannot be overstated. There are seven visible heavenly bodies which move across the stars and which daily or nightly rise at various positions in the east and curve overhead to the south to set in the west. Each used to be imagined as having its own shell, or sphere, around the earth. Walking a seven-coil labyrinth hints at a journey to Earth (the centre) via these seven heavenly bodies.

THE WALLS OF TROY

Rockcliffe Marsh in Cumbria used to have a number of turf labyrinths. The beautiful design shown right was copied and drawn in 1883 when it was still visible by R. Ferguson. Sadly, all have now vanished.

This pattern measured 24 by 26 feet with paths and gaps each about 8 or 9 inches wide. There are five coils wrapped round each side and eight coils vertically from the centre. Five and eight are, incidentally, two numbers which are often found to operate together. A three-coil heart-shaped spiral must finally be walked before oscillating three times backwards and forwards over the centre.

This type of labyrinth, combining spiral and oscillating themes, is more commonly found in Scandinavian countries where they were often associated with protection from depressing and clingy spirits of the dead. These poor lost souls reputedly could only travel in dead straight lines (down old spirit paths, or ley lines) and so would get caught in the coils of these wonderful forms when the possessed human walked them. It is probably for this rather spooky reason that the folk name for a labyrinth in many countries is still 'Spirit Trap'.

TARRY TOWN

Two miles outside Oxford lies the village of Temple Cowley and here used to be found the most simple labyrinth in the country. The Order of the Knights Templar were once the landowners, and the members of this secretive body used to walk the path as part of their initiations. The labyrinth was destroyed in 1852.

This was the only example of a four-circuit labyrinth known anywhere in the British Isles; it measured sixteen and a half feet across.

As in all good labyrinths the walker initially heads straight for the centre but is diverted on a much longer journey in the process. A useful rhyme elaborating on this theme was reputedly recited by folk walking this design:

So my boy, you wish to marry,
'Twere better far for you to tarry.
Each one's load's enough to carry,
And it's doubled when you marry.

CAWDOR CASTLE

Far from being a dead art, maze and labyrinth building fever has gripped the country for quite a few years now. The design shown opposite is a good example. Originally a Roman mosaic design from Conimbriga in Portugal, it can now be found as a hedge labyrinth at Cawdor Castle, in Nairnshire, Scotland, where it was planted in 1981.

The form is known as a double-meander, which means that each quarter requires the walker to zig-zag twice within it before moving on to the next quarter. There are no circum-navigatory paths and, unusually, the walker is repeatedly presented with his or her proximity to the centre before finally getting there.

If you fold up the design like a fan from the bottom (*see page 21*), you get the pattern below.

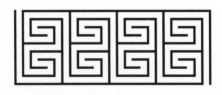

HARPHAM

The Romans were keen labyrinth builders and designs were adapted and generated to suit their tradition of mosaic flooring. Five Roman labyrinths have been found in the British Isles to date and the one shown opposite is from Harpham in Yorkshire. Measuring eleven feet across it is dated to 304 AD and can now be seen at the City Hall of Kingston-upon-Hull in Humberside.

The design is known as a triple-meander, the quadrants each containing three repeats being completed in an anticlockwise order. A similar Roman labyrinth found at Caerleon in Gwent can be seen in the Caerleon Museum. It too is a triple-meander but, unusually, the journey is clockwise.

The word *labyrinth* is obscure. It may or may not be relevant that the *Labrys*, the double-headed axe carried on a bundle of rods by Roman youths and carved into one of the stones at Stonehenge, has a shape roughly similar to the classical brain labyrinth (*next page*).

THE CITY OF TROY

On the verge beside the B1363 from Dalby to Terrington in Yorkshire can be found the only turf version of the traditional seven-coil labyrinth in the British Isles. The present cutting dates from the turn of the century. Labyrinths often go by the name of 'Troy' and a more likely explanation than a horse lies in the fact that the Welsh *Caerdroia*, meaning 'the walls (or city) of Troy' can also be taken as *Caer y troiau*, which means *The City of Turns.*

Examples of this classical labyrinth design occur right across the ancient world and are found on old Cretan coins, and carved on walls from Mexico to Spain, from India to Ireland.

If the seven planets visible planets are superimposed in their traditional order (*see page 36*) then the journey goes as follows: Mars is the first circuit to be walked (*"I Will have a go at the mysteries"*), then Jupiter (*"Wow! Cosmic! So much!"*), then Saturn (*"Time to learn the Rulebook"*), then the circuit of the Sun (*Glow! Lesser Mysteries complete"*), then the Moon (*"Give it back, reflect it"*), Mercury (*"How? Communicate it"*), and finally Venus (*"With love and beauty"*).

TROY TOWN

This labyrinth, at Somerton in Oxfordshire, is the only fifteen-coil classical labyrinth in the British Isles. Roughly sixty feet across, it sits in the grounds of Troy Farm beside the ancient Portway track.

The route takes the walker straight to the central cross and then requires the completion of the seven outer coils before the crossing is reached again. The seven inner coils are then walked before the aspirant can reach the sanctuary.

The geometry of this shape, and indeed that of all similar labyrinths, is strangely close to that of the common type-B flattened stone circle, examples of which litter ancient Britain. It has also been shown that there are many examples of concordance between this shape and the changing horizon positions of the rising and setting Sun, Moon and planets in their journeyings round the Earth.

There are fifteen circuits here, possibly reflecting the fifteen spheres of medieval cosmology. These were, starting at the centre, the four elemental spheres, then the seven planetary spheres, and finally the four highest heavenly spheres (*see page 54 for more detail*).

THE MIZ MAZE

The only square labyrinth to have survived from antiquity is the nine-circuit Miz Maze on St. Catherine's Hill, overlooking Winchester. Just under ninety feet wide it has a cut pathway - as opposed to the pathway being the raised dragon's-back of turf itself, the cuts separating the coils.

St. Catherine's Hill was fortified in the Iron Age, remained sacred in Roman times and was still the associated Holy Hill of the town when Winchester flourished as the largest ecclesiastical centre north of Rome in the twelfth century. St. Catherine, like St. Michael and St. George is associated with dragon-slaying, and hills where there are also springs. A small chapel once stood near the Maze.

A mere arrow's throw from St. Catherine's Hill is the even more ancient Twyford Down on which the Kings of Wessex were crowned and where the 'Dongas', the 8000 year-old system of ancient trackways of the entire south-east of the island used to meet. Sadly this ancient and wonderful place has recently been bulldozed for our grandchildren. Twyford Down is simply not there anymore, it has become a colossal cutting for a motorway, but, nearby, nine coils remain.

HERBAL LABYRINTH

This design appeared in a book by one Thomas Hyll in 1563. Entitled *A Most Briefe and Pleasaunt Treatyse Teachynge How to Dress, Sowe and Set a Garden*, the book contains two of Hyll's designs. During the 15th and 16th centuries labyrinths became extremely fashionable. The renaissance had not yet progressed to its expedient conclusion and some metaphysical advice still remained - here Hyll advised the careful planting of herbs according to the scheme of the seven visible heavenly bodies in their traditional order.

Earth is the central space, and then, moving out, the circuits represent the Moon, Mercury, Venus, Sun, Mars, Jupiter and Saturn, the order given by their speeds of motion against the stars. Sadly nowadays the Sun, like Brussels, is the remote centre and few understand the heavens. A version, shown below, once existed at Theobalds in Hertfordshire.

WATTS MEMORIAL CHAPEL

This labyrinth can be found inside the Watts Memorial Chapel, Compton, Surrey. It is a copy of the famous seven-circuit pavement labyrinth at San Vitale, Ravenna in Italy.

The Chapel was built in 1896 by Mary Watts to her husband and is heavily influenced by the ideas of William Lethaby whose *Architecture, Mysticism and Myth* (1891) had argued persuasively for the reunion of the fine crafts with meta-physical studies. It was due to Lethaby, William Morris and other luminaries of the day that the Royal College of Art came into existence. Sadly little or no traditional meta-physics is taught in such places today, spawning an entire generation of artists and designers who have never heard of the seven heavens - let alone the golden section.

After a familiar initial dash at the centre the path wanders from the innermost coil outwards and inwards through coils one, two and three before processing out through all the coils to the seventh. From here the path moves slowly back in to the fifth coil, then out again to the seventh. Finally the way moves inwards coil by coil until, from the third, Venus again, the centre is suddenly found.

BATHEASTON

In 1985 this fascinating labyrinth was laid in the parish church of Batheaston near Bath. Measuring 16' 6" across, the subgrid is forty-nine by forty-nine squares. Forty-nine is the square of seven, traditionally associated with Venus, which makes the subgrid seven by seven seven by sevens, or a Venus square of Venus squares.

The pattern is a copy of the medieval labyrinth, 44' 6" wide, which used to exist at the abbey of St. Bertin, Saint-Omer, Pas-de-Calais in France.

The medieval Venus square is shown below with odd numbers reversed (*to see why, turn to page 58*). All rows and columns add up to 175 (5 x 5 x 7).

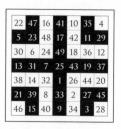

HARLEY MANUSCRIPT

This charming labyrinth appears in a tiny book amongst the Harley manuscripts in the British Museum. There is an excellent balance between the strong cross motif and the circular and diagonal elements.

Like many Roman designs, this labyrinth requires the person travelling it to complete each quarter in turn. The first three quarters are characterised by a long dash at the centre, followed by a sideways bounce all the way back out again. The quarters are zig-zagged from the outside in, and then from the inside out again before each mad dash - with the exception of the fourth quarter: This is covered from the inside out before zig-zagging back in to the circuit of Venus, Love and Beauty, from where the centre is won.

Thus three headlong runs at the central temenos are gently deflected whilst one carefully planned approach is rewarded.

43

PIMPERNE

This unique and unusual labyrinth once existed at Pimperne in Dorset, near Blandford. It was ploughed up in 1730, but was luckily recorded by the well-known antiquarian John Aubrey. Cut into the turf, the path was bounded by one foot hight ridges. Writing in 1686, Aubrey states that it was "... much used by the young people on Holydaies and by ye School-boies."

The essentially triangular design is unique in Great Britain, as is the spagetti-like nature of the coiling. The only clue to its function is the tiny heart-shaped island at the centre, a reminder of the true purpose of life to any walker. The 'corners' are completed in an anticlockwise direction, starting with the bottom-left.

Having reached the centre, and stepping off the path, a further challenge could have presented itself here - finding a way out without crossing the path, possibly a useful trick for avoiding gremlins left behind in the coils.

THE SHEPHERD'S RING

Thirty-seven feet across, this labyrinth once existed on the Green of Boughton village, near Northampton. It was destroyed by soldiers practising trench-building for the first world war in 1917.

The Ring seems to have been run every year during the Midsummer Fair, which lasted three days and nights, and which had been held there at least from 1353 when it was granted by Edward III. Exhausted ring-runners, wrestlers and revellers would be refreshed and sobered-up from the nearby St. John's Spring as the festivities peaked on St. John's Eve, the 23rd June.

The design is a variant on the medieval 11-coil labyrinth (*see page 54-57*) with the outer eight circuits following the standard pattern while the inner three simply form an elegant spiral. Thus the eleven is naturally divided into three and eight.

SAFFRON WALDEN

The largest ancient labyrinth in the British Isles can still be seen in Saffron Walden, Essex. It is surrounded by a ditch and ring mound and measures about 120 feet across. The pathway is one mile long and there used to be a tree on the central mound. As at the St. Catherine's Hill Mizmaze, the path consists of the groove instead of the raised turf.

The four corner protrusions were known as 'bastions' and point towards the nearby market towns of Newmarket, Chelmsford, Bishop's Stortford and Cambridge. The design is unique, having 17 circuits. Legend has it that an even larger labyrinth once existed further to the east.

As at many other labyrinths there used to be a custom that a maiden would stand at the centre while her beau would try and run the whole design without putting a foot wrong. Legends then vary: some say he was allowed to dance with her, but others recount that he had to carry her all the way out of the labyrinth if he wished to keep her - and this could have been no small task at Saffron Walden.

ROBIN HOOD S RACE

This ancient labyrinth used to sit on the summit of a hill near St. Anne's holy well, Sneinton, from which, it is recorded, flowed the purest and most healing water in all Nottinghamshire. The entrance seems to have been in the west.

The pathway was, like Saffron Walden, a trench between raised turf banks and was said to be 535 yards long; the design was also measured at one hundred feet across. The corner bastions contained crosses, crosslets or 'fitchies' cut into the turf.

Robin Hood's Race was ploughed up in 1797 as the new enclosures removed common rights to common land from common people, a process which is still in vogue all over the world.

The design is a slight variation on the medieval eleven-circuit pattern (*see pages 54-57*) with a quick exit route - or, if you want to cheat, a fast entrance!

ELY CATHEDRAL

In 1870 this labyrinth was laid in the pavement under the west tower of Ely Cathedral in Cambridgeshire. As in the case of the medieval labyrinth at Chartres Cathedral (*see page 56*) the length of the winding pathway is the same as the length of the cathedral.

The design is peculiar to Ely and was the work of Sir Gilbert Scott. A five-circuit dynamic square with protruding three-circuit octagons, it bears no similarity to any known medieval labyrinth.

The tradition of having labyrinths in the west end of cathedrals is prevalent in France where priests would dance their way to the centre, three steps at a time, having first formed a chain. The dean went first, occasionally throwing a large ball to priests caught elsewhere in the labyrinth who would then throw it back to him. The ball seems to have symbolised the Sun, or possibly the Moon, both newly hidden behind huge stone buildings.

British monks also walked mazes and labyrinths, but more often as penances, or allegorical pilgrimages.

THE SHOEMAKERS RACE

This turf labyrinth was first cut by the Patriotic Company of Shoemakers at Kingsland, near Shrewsbury, in 1598 but was destroyed in 1796 to make space for a windmill. On reaching the centre the walker or runner is reported to have had to jump on to 'the Giant's Head', a great green face cut into the central turf, with one heel in each eye.

The design is an octagonal version of the medieval eleven-circuit labyrinth. Eleven was the total number of spheres in the medieval cosmos. In addition to the seven spheres of the heavenly bodies (*see page 36*) four more outer spheres were indicated - the sphere of the fixed stars (the stations), the sphere of the sky without stars (the zodiacal signs), the sphere of the Divine Pedestal and the sphere of the Divine Throne. These four outer spheres were sometimes balanced by four inner elemental spheres - Ether, Air, Water and Earth, making fifteen in all (*see page 32*). Eleven and seven, the two most common labyrinth numbers, also relate to each other as the perimeter of a semicircle does to its width, thus again relating the line and the curve.

A twelve-sided, 40' version of this design also once existed between the villages of Paul and Marfleet in Yorkshire.

THE 11-COIL LABYRINTH

The most famous eleven-coil medieval labyrinth is on the floor of Chartres Cathedral near Paris, the same size as the huge window above it. There are quite a few turf versions still left in Great Britain. One, measuring 55 feet across, is on the village green of Hilton, Cambridgeshire. Another, 50 feet wide, can be seen at Wing in Leicestershire. A particularly famous version, called Julian's Bower, overlooks the spot where the rivers Trent and Humber meet near Alkborough, Humberside. Another lovely example is to be found at Braemore, near Salisbury, where the labyrinth sits in a clearing deep in sleepy woodland.

There are 28 half-moon turns, and four quarter-turns in the design; the folded version is shown below (*see pages 20-21*).

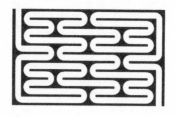

FROM THE CROSS TO THE CURVE

One way of unifying the line and the curve was shown on page 20; another is shown below.

A cross form is drawn. Offset arcs are then constructed from left to right over and around the cross as shown - just keep joining the dots and ends. This is the most simple method of drawing the classical seven coil labyrinth and is easily mastered after a few attempts on the back of an envelope.

Thus a 'Templar' cross, with links to the 7 by 7 Venus square (*see page 40*) and the 9 by 9 square of the Moon, quickly and easily produces the traditional 7-coil labyrinth.